Exploring Government Student Review

Student Review Material Prepared by
Ray Notgrass, Charlene Notgrass, and Nate McCurdy

Literary Analysis by Ray Notgrass and Bethany Poore

Exploring Government Student Review
ISBN: 978-1-60999-104-3

Cover Image Credits:
Morgan County, Georgia, Courthouse by Sean Pavone / Shutterstock.com;
Blue background by ksusha_art / Shutterstock.com

Cover design by Mary Evelyn McCurdy
Interior design by Charlene Notgrass

Printed in the United States of America

Notgrass Company
1-800-211-8793
www.notgrass.com

A Note to Parents

The *Exploring Government Student Review Pack* is a tool to measure your student's progress as they study *Exploring Government*. It includes three books: the *Student Review*, the *Quiz and Exam Book*, and an *Answer Key*. This material is intended to enhance your student's study of government. Please do not let it become a burden. Students should focus on learning about government, as they enjoy the literature and the primary documents and grow in their understanding of God's will concerning government and the way government is and has been practiced, especially in the United States. We pray you and your student have a successful study of government!

Student Review

The material in the *Student Review* is arranged in the order in which a student will come to it as they study the course. The assignment box at the end of each lesson in Exploring Government prompts your student as to when to complete the material in this book.

Review Questions. The *Student Review* includes review questions on each lesson, plus questions over each of the four literature titles we suggest students read as they study Exploring Government. Many parents require their students to write out answers to these questions on paper or on a computer; however, that is certainly not required. Other parents and students discuss the questions orally, and some parents use them for family discussion. If your student writes the answers on paper, we suggest that he or she answer them in a spiral notebook or on notebook paper which he keeps in a three-ring binder. These answers will be helpful for studying for quizzes and exams.

Literary Analysis. We love good books. We have carefully selected the literature titles that are assigned with this course. If you want your student simply to read and enjoy the books, we think that is wonderful. If you would like them to dig a little deeper and analyze the literature, you can have your student read the literature questions and literary analyses we have include in this book. The activities at the end of the lessons in the *Exploring Government* text will tell the student when to answer the questions and read the analyses. As we said above, please do not let any of this material become a burden.

After this Note to Parents, we have included "What Do You Think About What He Thinks? A Primer for Analysis of Non-Fiction" (to be read after Lesson 1). Your student will be given a reminder when it is time for him or her to read this section.

Quiz and Exam Book

The *Quiz and Exam Book* contains a quiz over each unit and also comprehensive exams that cover five units each. The assignment box at the end of each lesson in *Exploring Government* prompts your student to take a quiz at the end of each unit and to take the comprehensive exams after every five units. Each of these exams includes material from the previous five units. The quizzes and exams have been designed so that you can tear out one at a time and have your student write directly on that piece of paper.

Preparing for Quizzes. To prepare for a unit quiz, the student should look back over the review questions for the lessons from that unit.

Preparing for Exams. To prepare for the comprehensive exams, the student should review the quizzes and answers from each of the previous five units.

Answer Key

The *Answer Key* contains the answers to the review questions, quizzes, and exams, as well as the answers to questions about the literature. The number in parentheses after an answer indicates the page number on which that answer is found in *Exploring Government*.

What Do You Think About What He Thinks?
A Primer for Analysis of Non-Fiction

A non-fiction article, essay, or book will likely make an argument, teach, or convey information. Of course, a work of fiction might also be an attempt to make an argument, teach, or convey information; but a non-fiction work presents the information and the author's perspective in a straightforward manner. The non-fiction piece might be in the form of a story; but it is a story from real life, as with a biography.

Part of education is considering perspectives other than your own and developing your response to them. In a persuasive work, a writer has something to say that he hopes others will at least consider and perhaps agree with. Even the author of a biography writes for a purpose, not only to inform but perhaps also to convince readers about something regarding his subject: that he was instrumental in a war, or influential in Congress, or had some other significant impact.

By reading a work of non-fiction, you might be confirmed in what you believe about something or you might be convinced that you need to change your opinion. You might obtain more information that helps you have a more realistic perspective on an issue. You shouldn't fear this process. You don't want to cast aside basic truth and fall for every new idea you hear, but part of growing and maturing is gaining a more complete understanding of truth. No one has a grasp of all truth or the perfect application of that truth in every situation. Everyone can grow in some areas of life, whether that means learning more truth or learning how to apply the truth you know to more situations. This process is part of growing in what the Bible calls discernment (see Hebrews 5:13-14).

A text can be any written material. We analyze every text that we read, whether it is an encyclopedia article, a book of political commentary, or an advertisement, even if only briefly and subconsciously. We don't want to lose the joy of reading by over-analyzing, but it is good to do serious and conscious analysis for several reasons. Analysis will help you understand the meaning and purpose of a text; you might even discern a meaning beneath the surface. It can help you connect the text with its background, such as the time in which it was written or something about the author. You can profitably compare the text with other texts to see which are more consistent and believable. Analyzing a text can help you prove a thesis. A summary of a text is a report of its content, but an analysis of a text is an evaluation of its meaning and significance.

In analyzing a work of non-fiction, you want to ask questions of the text. You probably won't address every question below about every text, but here are things to consider when analyzing non-fiction:

- What is the author's point or purpose?
- What is the argument he is making?
- What is the motivation for the piece? What problem does it address?
- What evidence or logic does he use to support his thesis?

- What is the context from which the author writes (time, place, point of view, background and experience)?
- What assumptions does the author bring to writing this piece?
- What words or ideas are repeated? These will often be clues to the author's point.
- What word choices seem significant? Does the author use any figures of speech to make his argument more persuasive?
- What is the structure of the text (for example, autobiography, memoir, or examination of a particular subject)? How does the author build his argument through the work? How does the structure help make the author's point?
- What are the key passages in the work, and why are they important?
- What is surprising, odd, or troubling in the text? (These parts are likely challenging your current understanding.)
- What contradictions and inconsistencies do you find in the text?
- What assumptions do you bring to the text?
- Is the text convincing to you? Why or why not? (It is entirely likely that you will agree with some things and disagree with other parts.)
- What questions do you have after reading it? What further study do you need to do?

When you write an analysis of a non-fiction work, gather your information, impressions, and answers to these questions, then write a coherent essay that responds to the piece. Depending on the length of your essay, you will probably want to summarize the author's purpose and argument, emphasize the central points as you see them, note where you think the author is correct and where he is mistaken, and where he is effective and where he could have expressed his ideas differently. Keep in mind the nature of your assignment, what the teacher expects from you, and what the reader of your analysis needs to understand about the work you are analyzing and about your response to it.

The author whose work you have read wants you to think. Show that you have thought. Expressing your thoughts on paper indicates how well you understand what he has said and, more importantly, how well you understand your own thoughts about the subject.

Unit 1

Lesson 1

1. With whom did the idea of government originate?
2. Why did Claudius order all Jews to leave Rome?
3. How does Paul describe human rulers?
4. Since government authority is from God, how does Paul instruct Christians to relate to government?
5. What does Paul say in Romans 13 are two important functions of government?
6. According to 1 Peter 2:11, how do Christians live in this world?
7. What does Daniel 2:21 teach about God's rule over the whole world?
8. What did Mary say about rulers in Luke 1:52?
9. When government issued ungodly directives, what did Peter and the apostles say they must do?
10. According to Titus 2:14, what are Christians to do; and according to Matthew 5:13-16, what are Christians to be?

Lesson 2

1. What did John Adams say free government rests upon?
2. What is the most important form of human government?
3. What is the basis of the immense worth of every individual?
4. The lesson names what principle of the civil rights movement of the 1950s and 1960s?
5. The Bible says that government leaders have a responsibility to see that the government does what?
6. What did the prophet Amos tell the people of Israel to do?
7. We learn from Amos that justice is above what?
8. Why did Israel and Judah fall?
9. What did the concept of the divine right of kings hold about the power of a king?
10. What does Proverbs teach about the permanence of dynasties?

Lesson 3

1. What are the basic principles of the Law which God gave to Moses?
2. According to the Ten Commandments, who or what is the basis for life?
3. What does the word holy mean?
4. Why should Christians be holy in their lives?
5. The weakening of what, either by accepted practice or by law, will weaken society and its government?
6. What character trait is essential for society to operate well?
7. How are God's people to view life?
8. How should God's people view the property of others?
9. The Law of Moses considered a person to be innocent until what?
10. What punishment common in American justice is absent in the Law of Moses?

Lesson 4

1. People in positions of leadership carry great what?
2. What kind of men was Moses to appoint to hear disputes among the Israelites?
3. Why did Moses need to appoint men with these characteristics?
4. Why was a king not to acquire many horses, wives, or much wealth?
5. How was a king to show his dependence on the Law?
6. Who was the person described as the "man after God's own heart"?
7. What does Proverbs say about the mouth of a king?
8. What does Proverbs say about the influence that a king and his advisers can have on each other?
9. In what ways does Ezekiel say that the shepherds of Israel had failed their sheep?
10. If you were a governmental leader, what Biblical principles would you use in your position?

Lesson 5

1. As best we can tell, what was the pattern of government in the ancient world?
2. What was the pattern of community leadership in Israel?
3. Whom did God want to rule over Israel?
4. How did God plan to provide leaders for Israel?
5. What motivated the Israelites' desire for a king to rule over them?
6. What revolt gave the Jews a measure of freedom and self-government?
7. Of the three branches of government (legislative, executive, and judicial), which did the Sanhedrin fulfill?
8. From where did the members of the Jewish Sanhedrin come?
9. Why were the leading officials of Philippi deferential to Paul and Silas?
10. Who blamed Christians for the great fire in Rome in 64 AD and began active persecution of the church?

Unit 2

Lesson 6

Define these terms:

1. state
2. government
3. sovereignty
4. dictatorship
5. oligarchy
6. constitutional monarchy
7. republic
8. democracy
9. state religion
10. limited government

Lesson 7

1. Throughout history, who has been the most common head of government for almost every culture and ethnic group?
2. List five ways in which a man became a king.
3. What was commonly demonstrated by the amount of land a king owned?
4. List four reasons a king might go to war against another land.
5. Who made up the king's council of advisers?
6. With what two things did lords and barons support a king they trusted?
7. What individual was a major influence on kings during the Middle Ages?
8. What was the greatest threat the pope could use to influence a king?
9. Who was usually a king's heir?
10. Would you want to be an absolute monarch? Explain your answer.

Lesson 8

1. What ancient Greek city-state developed the form of government we call democracy?
2. What was the name of the law-making meeting of Athenian citizens?
3. What was the meaning of the Greek word *idiotes* from which we get our word idiot?
4. In general, individual rights in Athens had less value than what?
5. What was the result of the practice of Athenians selecting leaders by lot?
6. What was the ruling body in the Roman Republic?
7. Define patrician and plebeian.
8. How did plebeians change government over time in the Roman Republic?
9. The Senate's recognition of whom as emperor is seen as beginning the Roman Empire?
10. Rather than ensuring popular control of government, what was the purpose of the Roman Senate?

Lesson 9

1. What was a witenagemot?
2. How did English government change after William of Normandy invaded in 1066?
3. What did the English barons force King John to sign in 1215?
4. What did the council meeting that was formed when Henry III repudiated this agreement come to be called?
5. Why do historians refer to the meeting called by King Edward I in 1295 as the Model Parliament?
6. Where did most government functions that affected most of the people take place in the 1630s in England?
7. The theory of royal authority believed in by James I of England was called what?
8. Who abolished the monarchy after Charles I was executed in 1649?
9. In effect, Robert Walpole began to serve in what role in 1721?
10. What three things did English colonists in America see in the government of the United Kingdom that they did not want to repeat in America?

Lesson 10

1. What philosophical movement helped to mold the thinking of the men who shaped our American system?
2. What did the Enlightenment exalt as the best basis for understanding life and the world?
3. Scholars see the period of the Enlightenment beginning with the publication of what in 1687?
4. What did Enlightenment writers start questioning about kings?
5. What term did John Locke use to describe how people associate with each other?
6. What did John Locke believe was the reason people decided to associate with each other in a social contract?
7. What kind of government did Locke believe produced the most freedom for people?
8. What did Locke say that people have a right to do if government threatens their rights?
9. Baron de Montesquieu wrote that government should be divided into what three branches?
10. How do you believe the Enlightenment fostered the idea of "self-evident truths"?

Unit 3

Lesson 11

1. What were three common elements of colonial government?
2. Who chose the elected assembly in a colony?
3. How did George III respond after the French and Indian War?
4. Why was the New England Confederation formed in 1643?
5. What was the purpose of the Albany meeting in 1754?
6. When colonial representatives met in New York in October 1765, they protested what they saw as unjust taxation without what?
7. Why did the First Continental Congress meet in 1774?
8. What had happened by the time the Second Continental Congress met in 1775?
9. In 1776 Richard Henry Lee of Virginia proposed a resolution in the Continental Congress that the colonies ought to be what?
10. The Declaration of Independence states that government derives its power from what?

Lesson 12

1. What new institution did many states convene after they became independent?
2. What is the world's oldest founding document still in use?
3. What was the main purpose of the Articles of Confederation?
4. How many votes did each state have in the Confederation Congress?
5. What provision did the Articles make for a national executive and a national court system?
6. What did the Northwest Ordinance do concerning territories and new states?
7. What was the result of the Articles of Confederation requiring nine votes to pass significant laws?
8. What realities caused concern about the strength of the United States in relation to foreign countries?
9. What meeting proposed a revision of the Articles?
10. Where did most Americans want political power to remain?

Lesson 13

1. In what year did the Constitutional Convention meet?
2. What policy did the delegates follow regarding publicity?
3. What was the compromise reached about the make-up of Congress?
4. What did the compromise regarding the office of president involve?
5. What was the compromise reached about slavery?
6. What did most Americans believe about the strength of the central government?
7. What is the meaning of the term "delegated powers"?
8. Explain how the Constitution separates powers in relation to the military.
9. What have the newspaper articles James Madison, Alexander Hamilton, and John Jay wrote to encourage that the Constitution be adopted come to be called?
10. What are the four reasons the lesson lists to explain why the Constitution has been successful?

Lesson 14

1. What did the Founding Fathers want and expect to be a vital part of American life?
2. Freedom of religion is guaranteed in which amendment to the Constitution?
3. Describe the role of religion in the founding of the United States.
4. What two principles did the new nation follow in matters of religion?
5. What did Congress call for immediately after passing the First Amendment in 1789?
6. Where does the lesson mention that both Presidents Thomas Jefferson and James Madison attended church services?
7. What are some examples of the beliefs of the Founding Fathers?
8. In what founding documents is God mentioned?
9. What did most people in the new nation believe about God?
10. Which colony did Rogers Williams found with the purpose of having more complete religious liberty?

Lesson 15

1. The Preamble of the Constitution states that American government begins with whom?
2. How does the Preamble express the idea of a covenant?
3. How many of the writers of the Constitution were immigrants or descendants of immigrants?
4. How did the Constitution form a more perfect union?
5. How did the Constitution establish justice?
6. Why did the Constitution need to ensure domestic tranquility?
7. What is the meaning of the phrase "provide for the common defense"?
8. What is the meaning of the phrase "the general welfare"?
9. What two specific applications have been made of the Preamble's reference to "our posterity"?
10. The people of one generation have what responsibility to those who come after them?

Unit 4

Lesson 16

1. Why is such a large portion of the Constitution devoted to Congress?
2. What are the constitutional qualifications for serving in the House?
3. What is the length of a congressman's term in office?
4. How is a House seat filled that is made vacant by death or resignation?
5. The number of congressmen a state sends to the House of Representatives is based on what?
6. The permanent size of the House of Representatives is how many members?
7. What is apportionment and how often does reapportionment take place?
8. Who is responsible for drawing the district lines for a state?
9. What is gerrymandering and what is the origin of the term?
10. Name at least two guidelines that Congress and the courts have established for how legislatures should pursue redistricting.

Lesson 17

1. Why is the Senate considered the upper house of Congress?
2. What are the constitutional qualifications for serving in the Senate?
3. Why is the Senate considered to be a continuing body?
4. How were senators chosen in the original Constitution?
5. How did this change on a national basis?
6. How has the popular election of senators affected the power of state legislatures?
7. What is the most common way for a Senate seat to be filled when it is made vacant by death or resignation?
8. What is meant by the advice and consent role of the Senate?
9. Does the president have the right to remove an appointee without the Senate's approval?
10. What is a recess appointment?

Lesson 18

1. In what two ways is the word Congress used in American government?
2. The meetings of Congress in a given year are called a what?
3. In the original Constitution, when did Congress convene; and what are the modern dates for the convening of Congress and the president's inauguration?
4. When does a lame duck session of Congress occur?
5. What happens when a senator or a representative requests a quorum call?
6. What publication reports the proceedings of the House and the Senate?
7. What did C-SPAN begin telecasting in 1979?
8. Define franking privilege.
9. When Congress votes itself a pay raise, when can it go into effect?
10. When is a senator or representative immune from being arrested?

Lesson 19

1. Why is it unusual for a salaried or wage-earning man or woman to be elected to Congress?
2. What is a safe seat?
3. What is a freshman member of Congress?
4. Define term limits.
5. What is the most obvious work that a senator or congressman does?
6. Name two things a senator or congressman might do for a constituent.
7. What is a junket?
8. What is a congressional delegation trip?
9. What former president sold his extensive library to Congress?
10. Where must applicants for official copyright send copies of their work?

Lesson 20

1. What type of faction or group did many of the Founding Fathers fear?
2. Early representatives and senators who favored a strong central government took what name?
3. Those who favored limiting the central government and who promoted the power of the states took what name?
4. What two political parties that formed before the Civil War continue to be the most powerful today?
5. Name the four political party leaders in both the House and Senate.
6. How is the speaker of the House chosen?
7. Who is the official president of the Senate?
8. What office did the framers of the Constitution create to preside in the Senate in the absence of the vice president?
9. What do House and Senate committees do?
10. Who chooses all of the committee chairmen?

See page 10 for literary analysis of and questions over *Mornings on Horseback*.

Literary Analysis
Mornings on Horseback
by David McCullough

A person is shaped by a complex set of influences that begins even before he or she is born. Ethnicity, faith, culture, economic status, education, birth order, health, values, parents, siblings, grandparents, and family history impact a person's life in a complex way that is somewhat impossible but entirely fascinating to explore. Who are your influences? What shapes you?

A standard biography includes the entire life of the subject, from birth to death. Why does *Mornings on Horseback* conclude just as Theodore Roosevelt really came into his own?

David McCullough's purpose in writing *Mornings on Horseback* was not to produce a biography of the 26th president, but to show how Roosevelt came to be who he was. The book's subtitle says it: "The Story of an Extraordinary Family, a Vanished Way of Life, and the Unique Child Who Became Theodore Roosevelt." This is a worthwhile task because Roosevelt was such a fascinating and complex person. *Mornings on Horseback* is a book about influences.

The expectations, standards, and values of the privileged, aristocratic Roosevelt clan and the well-established, highly respected Bulloch family were the foundations of influence in Theodore Roosevelt's life. The fact that the Roosevelts were longtime New Yorkers while the Bulloch family came from Deep South Georgia brought complex influences to Roosevelt's life.

Theodore Roosevelt's immediate family shaped one another. The Roosevelt siblings were close as children and into adulthood to an uncommon degree. His long-unmarried sister Bamie felt she had a special claim and a special responsibility on her famous brother. How do you think she influenced his decisions? Roosevelt's sister Corinne, his brother Elliot, and he were the best of friends and companions. How did they help to make him into the man he became? How do you think Elliot's waywardness and failures in his adult life influenced his brother?

The Roosevelt children had few influences from outside their "set," not even from a school setting. They were surrounded by extended family, even within their home. Their playmates and friends were relatives and other members of the wealthy class. How did these people shape them?

Though raised in the city, Roosevelt was well-informed and enthusiastic about the natural world. How did his family provide for and encourage this passion? The very different locations in which young Roosevelt lived—New York, his family's vacation spots away from the city's bustle, the wilderness of Dakota Territory—each deeply influenced the values and priorities of Theodore Roosevelt. How would the family's long leisurely tour of Europe's great cities and later the Nile shape a young man?

Wealth and privilege influenced Roosevelt's life. He never wondered where a meal was coming from. He probably never worried about his father losing his job. His world was soaked in luxuries. What perspective does that upbringing give a person?

Roosevelt was forever changed by his battle with asthma. His intermittent but intense asthmatic flare-ups were traumatic. As a boy he was small and sickly. He wanted to take his place in the world as a strong, healthy, capable man; but for years his physical weakness held him back. His father exhorted him and gave him the tools and opportunity to do all he could to improve his health. How do you think Theodore Roosevelt was different as an adult because of these struggles when he was young?

Theodore's desire to make his father proud shaped his entire life well beyond wanting to follow his father's instructions for building up his body. Theodore Sr.'s influence reached to every corner of his son's world. The entire family adored Theodore Roosevelt Sr. They regarded him as a truly great man, almost as one regards a "saint." Theodore Sr. had every success that their privileged set desired, yet he had uncommon drive, intelligence, and kindness to those in need. After Theodore Sr. died when the younger Theodore was still in college, the son longed to live a life that would have made his father proud.

These complex influences poured into one man's life and changed history. From fighting in the Spanish-American War, the building of the Panama Canal, the creation of national parks, a long and eventful presidency, and the raising of a large, boisterous family, Theodore Roosevelt led "the strenuous life" he desired. He is known for his energy, passion, and strong opinions. He is one of the most interesting and colorful characters in American history.

Note about the Author

David McCullough is the most widely-read historian of our day. His books have sold millions of copies, have remained in print for years, and have been the basis for television programs and miniseries.

McCullough majored in English literature, not history, at Yale. He originally wanted to be a novelist, but he found his passion in writing history. He decided that he wanted to write books that he would enjoy reading, on subjects he wanted to learn about. He grew up in Pittsburgh, Pennsylvania, so his first book was about the Johnstown, Pennsylvania, flood of 1889. McCullough then became interested in how the Brooklyn Bridge was built. McCullough had walked across the bridge many times when he lived in New York.

His editor suggested a book on the Panama Canal, which was his next project. An offshoot of his study of that period was this book about Theodore Roosevelt. Moving to other presidential biographies, McCullough wrote *Truman* and then spent seven years writing *John Adams.* McCullough won the Pulitzer Prize for biography for both of these books. His research into John Adams helped lead to his book *1776,* which focused on George Washington and the difficult early days of the American Revolution. McCullough also wanted the book to encourage the nation after the 9/11 terrorist attacks. He has written several other books.

McCullough has composed his books on a 1941-vintage typewriter that he bought second-hand in 1964. He likes to say that he is not working on a book, but he is working in a book: getting to know the people and places, entering as personally as possible into the story he wants to share with others. He loves to do research, and he visits places he writes about so that he will have a better feel for his subjects.

Questions on *Mornings on Horseback*

Write about one page total to answer questions 1-3:

1. What are other influences in Theodore Roosevelt's life that we did not mention in the literary analysis?
2. What influences in Theodore Roosevelt's life can you relate to? How do similar influences impact your life?
3. List five values of Theodore Roosevelt's family that you think shaped him into a passionate leader.

Write about one-half to one page:

4. Write a summary and review of *Mornings on Horseback.*

Unit 5

Lesson 21

1. Where must revenue bills originate?
2. What four steps does the clerk perform when a representative puts a bill in the hopper or when a senator hands a bill to the clerk or makes a formal announcement to introduce it?
3. What are the four forms that legislation may take?
4. What is the difference between an authorization bill and an appropriation bill?
5. Give two examples of programs Congress considers to be mandatory.
6. Who has the most power in deciding which bills a committee will consider?
7. What happens in a markup session?
8. What does it mean for a bill to be "voted out"?
9. Who are lobbyists and what do they do?
10. If you worked as a lobbyist in Washington, what group would you want to represent? Why?

Lesson 22

1. Name three ways that one of the houses of Congress can vote on a bill.
2. When either the House or the Senate passes a bill, what happens next?
3. Where does a bill go if the second chamber makes any amendments to it?
4. What is a conference committee and what happens there?
5. What happens when a bill passes in the same form in both the House and the Senate?
6. What is a filibuster?
7. What is cloture?
8. What is an unfunded mandate?
9. How do political observers use the terms right and left when describing citizens who are conservative or liberal?
10. What are the three options that a president has when Congress passes a bill and sends it to him?

Lesson 23

1. What are duties and imposts?
2. Give three examples of items an American may have to pay an excise tax on when they purchase them.
3. What is the difference between the terms annual budget deficit and national debt?
4. In what realms is Congress authorized to regulate commerce?
5. What body has the power to declare war?
6. Why must military appropriations last no more than two years?
7. What are state militias now called?
8. What federal district does Congress govern?
9. What major role has the Supreme Court played in relation to the "Necessary and Proper" clause?
10. Who makes up the federal bureaucracy?

Lesson 24

1. What did the Constitution forbid before 1808?
2. What is a writ of habeas corpus?
3. What president suspended writs of habeas corpus in the name of maintaining order?
4. What is a bill of attainder?
5. What is an ex post facto law?
6. What amendment changed the taxes that Congress could impose?
7. What must happen before any money can be spent from the federal treasury?
8. Why did the framers of the Constitution forbid office holders to accept gifts, titles, offices, or money from foreign rulers or states?
9. What limitation does the Constitution place on states in regard to money?
10. What limitation does the Constitution place on states in regard to foreign governments?

Lesson 25

1. What does the term impeachment mean?
2. The Constitution's framers were familiar with the impeachment found where?
3. What is the role of the House in an impeachment case?
4. What is the role of the Senate in an impeachment case?
5. What does the phrase "high crimes and misdemeanors" mean?
6. What is the limit of penalty for being found guilty of impeachment charges?
7. What kind of officials have been impeached or investigated for impeachment?
8. What was the result when the Senate tried President Andrew Johnson after the House impeached him?
9. What president was impeached in connection with how he handled an investigation into his immorality?
10. What did President Richard Nixon do to avoid being impeached?

Unit 6

Lesson 26

1. What are the qualifications in the Constitution for becoming president?
2. What is the difference between a primary and a caucus?
3. Who is appointed at state conventions?
4. What two main things are decided upon at a national party convention?
5. What is the intended purpose of the Presidential Campaign Fund?
6. What was the original plan for how the electoral college was to work?
7. How did the 1800 election show the weakness of this approach?
8. How did the Twelfth Amendment change the system?
9. What do critics say about the electoral college?
10. What do supporters of the electoral college say?

Lesson 27

1. What is the average age of a president at the time of taking office?
2. What fraction of presidents have served in the military?
3. What phrase did George Washington add when he took the oath of office?
4. What was the salary set for the president as of 2016?
5. About how often between 1841 and 1963 did a president die in office?
6. What was a big question when William Henry Harrison died and John Tyler took the office?
7. Who is next in the line of succession after the vice president?
8. What prompted adoption of the Twenty-Fifth Amendment in 1967?
9. What provision does this amendment have for a president being disabled?
10. How often has a vice-presidential vacancy been filled by a nomination by the president?

Lesson 28

1. Why is civilian oversight of the U.S. armed forces important?
2. How is the war-making authority of the federal government an example of the separation of powers?
3. How many times has Congress declared war?
4. What did the Tonkin Gulf Resolution authorize the president to do?
5. In recent times, how has Congress authorized the president to deploy troops?
6. What law did Congress pass to limit a president's ability to deploy troops?
7. What prompted President Truman to send American troops into Korea in 1950?
8. What was significant about the targets of attack authorized by the passing of the AUMF in 2001?
9. What are two types of documents that a president might sign with leaders of other countries?
10. What is the term that describes the president's role in carrying on diplomatic relations with other countries?

Lesson 29

1. How many federal civilian employees work in the executive branch?
2. Once Congress establishes a program is it easy or difficult to end it?
3. How is the Pendleton Civil Service Act a double-edged sword?
4. What is the size of the president's personal and official staff?
5. Which president created the Executive Office of the president?
6. What three-member panel reports, reviews, and makes recommendations about the economy?
7. What body, made up of the vice president and some Cabinet officers, advises the president on foreign relations and other matters regarding safety for our country?
8. What tool can a president use to implement an agenda without waiting for Congress?
9. How might a president's agenda affect the way federal laws are executed?
10. What power of the president might be considered judicial?

Lesson 30

1. What happens when there is no majority in the electoral college?
2. How do the president and Congress work together to create laws?
3. What are the roles of Congress and the president concerning war?
4. What can Congress and the president do when Congress sends the president legislation he does not approve?
5. How has the initiative for legislation changed since the first years of the country?
6. What is the president's annual message to Congress?
7. What historic event in the mid-1800s resulted from a State of the Union address?
8. What might a president do to help his proposals get passed in Congress?
9. What is the term for when Congress and the president are hardened in their opposition to each other?
10. What is the idea of a presidential line-item veto and what happened after Congress passed a law giving that power to the president?

See page 16 for literary analysis of and questions over *The Autobiography of Calvin Coolidge.*

Literary Analysis
The Autobiography of Calvin Coolidge

Calvin Coolidge has received unfair treatment by the press, by most scholars, and in the understanding that people generally have of him. The usual perception of him is "Silent Cal," a man of few words who was merely a tool of big business and who stood by and let corporations ruin the country. This is grossly unfair, and it does not do justice to who he really was. His autobiography reveals Coolidge as a straightforward, hard-working public servant who had many wise insights into life and government.

What do you think was Coolidge's motivation for writing his autobiography? Surely he was ready for rest and privacy after his long years of public service, culminating in the presidency. Why would he choose to publish his autobiography right after leaving office? He must have had some specific reasons.

Wisdom. Writing in his late fifties, Coolidge had wisdom to share that he had gleaned from life experience. He skillfully navigated a path from a remote community in Vermont with a set pattern of life and a minimum of outside influences to Washington, D.C., a confluence of cultures and powerful people. His life experience was wide, yet he remained humble and unpretentious, always able to tell it like it is. The wisdom gleaned from such a life and such a man is worth giving and worth listening to.

History. Coolidge's autobiography reveals his sense of the history of which he was a part. He took the time to explain the roots of his family tree and their part in his making. He describes the world of his childhood, a simple yet rich way of life that he must have known was on the verge of disappearing. He shares his own memories of the historic events he was part of, from the police strike in Boston to the sudden death of President Harding in office. History carries depth of meaning from the viewpoint of a person who lived it.

Truth. The constant feed of information, true and false, about prominent people was a dynamic in the 1920s and has only increased since. Public service is so very public. People will have their opinions. To add their own voice to the swirl, many public servants and celebrities have written books with the purpose of informing the public, "OK, this is how it really was." The faintly defensive tone on certain topics reveals that Coolidge wanted his autobiography to set the record straight.

Honor. In telling his story, Coolidge took the time to honor the people who were important shapers of his life: his grandparents who read the Bible with him, the members of the community in which he was raised, his loving mother that he missed, his stepmother who was a blessing to him, his educators, his mentors in law and politics, his faithful wife, the son he lost at age sixteen, and above all, his father. In beautiful, grateful passages, Calvin Coolidge expresses his love for his father and the love he felt from his father. Not all "great men" become famous. This farmer/shopkeeper/public servant/president's father who lived his life in a tiny Vermont village had an important impact in history by the way he taught and cared for his son.

Exhortation. Through his wisdom, the stories he tells, the philosophies of life and government he shares, Calvin Coolidge exhorts his readers. Between the lines, he has some lessons he wants us to hear: Honor the quiet life of the country. Be grateful to the people who help you. Value education. Work hard. Don't be puffed up. Family is important. Serve your country. Do the right thing.

Story. Calvin Coolidge had a story to share, and those of us who read it are the better for it. Who doesn't love a story where the boy helping his dad in the barn in a remote village grows up to become the great man in the seat of power? Calvin Coolidge is the quintessential American success story. His life, like every life, is an important story. We can be thankful that he recognized the value of putting it on paper.

Wisdom from Calvin Coolidge

The silences of nature have a discipline all their own.

Country life does not always have breadth, but it has depth.

It seems to me that it is almost impossible for those who have not traveled that road [to learn about the ancient world] to reach a very clear conception of what the world now means.

[On the Constitution] No other document devised by the hand of man ever brought so much progress and happiness to humanity.

It is a great advantage to a president and a major source of safety of the country for him to know he is not a great man.

Questions on *The Autobiography of Calvin Coolidge*

Write about one page total to answer questions 1-3:

1. Why do you think the perception of Coolidge is so different from how he reveals himself in this book?
2. What contrasts do you see between Coolidge and the popular mindset of the 1920s?
3. What messages other than the ones we listed do you think Coolidge wanted the reader to take away?

Write about one-half to one page:

4. Write a summary and review of *The Autobiography of Calvin Coolidge.*

Unit 7

Lesson 31

1. The Constitution mentions heads of executive departments. What term do we use for that group of people today?
2. What department handles our relations with other countries?
3. Who was America's first secretary of State?
4. What are the two common ways that average Americans interact with the state department?
5. What was the Marshall Plan?
6. What department oversees the economic life of the nation?
7. What two entities does the Treasurer of the United States oversee?
8. What agency collects taxes within the United States?
9. What was the original name of the Defense Department under George Washington?
10. The highest ranking members of the U.S. military are called what?

Lesson 32

1. What is the title given to the head of the Justice Department?
2. Who serves as the government's representatives before the U.S. Supreme Court?
3. What do the letters FBI stand for and what is the responsibility of this agency within the Department of Justice?
4. What are the main functions of the Interior Department?
5. What is the purpose of the Bureau of Indian Affairs?
6. What is a controversial aspect of the Interior Department's responsibilities?
7. What does the Department of Agriculture do to foods that U.S. farmers produce and that importers bring into the country?
8. What agency within the Department of Agriculture administers the 4-H program?
9. What is a controversial area of the work of the Department of Agriculture?
10. Define parity.

Lesson 33

1. What does the Commerce Department gather and publish?
2. What is the purpose of the National Institute of Standards and Technology?
3. What are the purposes of the National Oceanic and Atmospheric Administration?
4. What is the main mission of the Labor Department?
5. Why did Congress create the Department of Housing and Urban Development?
6. What is the belief behind HUD's mission of encouraging home ownership?
7. List the nicknames of the three federally-chartered investment corporations involved in helping more money be available for home mortgages.
8. How is HUD involved in making rental property more available to the poor?
9. What is an infrastructure?
10. What percentage of highway construction costs does the federal government pay?

Lesson 34

1. What federal department accounts for about one-fourth of federal spending?
2. What are Medicare and Medicaid?
3. Who is the surgeon general?
4. What situation in the 1970s preceded the creation of the Energy Department?
5. What special interest group did politicians try to please by creating the Department of Education?
6. How has the Department of Education changed the oversight of the field of education?
7. What are some examples of benefits provided to military veterans?
8. What disaster prompted a rearranging of the federal government in 2001?
9. What are some agencies now in the Department of Homeland Security that had once been in other departments?
10. What agency leads the federal government's response to natural disasters?

Lesson 35

1. What independent agencies are under the oversight of Congress?
2. What was the first independent agency created by Congress?
3. What is America's central bank?
4. What independent agency insures the deposits that people have in banks?
5. What independent agency provides start-up loans for new businesses?
6. What three kinds of benefits does Social Security provide?
7. What independent agency oversees America's national space exploration program?
8. What is the function of the Central Intelligence Agency?
9. What independent agency maintains America's historic documents?
10. Give four examples of semi-private government corporations mentioned in Lesson 35.

Unit 8

Lesson 36

Define each term:

1. Magistrate
2. Bond money (bail money)
3. Grand jury
4. Indict
5. Plea bargain
6. Acquittal
7. Pre-trial discovery
8. Peremptory challenge
9. Parole
10. Appeals court

Lesson 37

1. What country's legal system was the primary basis for the American system?
2. What court did the Constitution establish?
3. What other federal courts has Congress created?
4. How are federal judges placed on the bench?
5. How long may federal judges serve?
6. In 2016 what was the salary of the Chief Justice of the Supreme Court?
7. What is the difference between criminal law and civil law?
8. Why do federal courts hear cases involving ambassadors, ministers, and consuls?
9. How is treason defined?
10. How many treason trials have taken place in the United States?

Lesson 38

1. What is the lowest court of the federal legal process?
2. What Senate committee holds hearings when a president nominates a federal judge?
3. How has politics affected Senate confirmation of judges?
4. What are four kinds of specialty federal courts?
5. The losing party in a federal district court case can appeal the verdict where?
6. Who heard appeals of cases in federal courts before Congress established the federal appeals court system?
7. How many justices usually hear a case in a federal circuit court of appeals?
8. What courts hear cases involving the military and veterans?
9. What is a senior federal judge?
10. Where can parties who have lost their appeals in the federal circuit courts of appeal file a further appeal?

Lesson 39

1. Why can it be said that the members of the U.S. Supreme Court are the most powerful persons in the federal government?
2. How many persons sit on the Supreme Court?
3. What is the average age of justices when *Exploring Government* was published?
4. Why are Supreme Court nominations so pivotal and so hotly debated?
5. What has come to be the primary function of the Supreme Court?
6. About how many appeals of cases does the Supreme Court receive each year?
7. About how many of those cases does the Court accept?
8. When does the Court's term begin?
9. What is the "conference handshake"?
10. What is the most important principle that guides the Court's deliberations?

Lesson 40

1. What did Franklin Roosevelt propose doing after the Supreme Court struck down several laws?
2. On what basis did the Supreme Court uphold the Social Security law in *Helvering v. Davis*?
3. How did Supreme Court decisions during the Great Depression expand the areas in which Congress passed laws?

4. What phrase came out of the *Plessy v. Ferguson* decision that upheld racial segregation?
5. Why did the Court rule in favor of Brown in the case of *Brown v. Board of Education*?
6. How did the *Brown v. Board of Education* decision reverse *Plessy*?
7. In what case did the Court say that certain procedures and safeguards for accused persons had to be in place?
8. Why did the Court rule in favor of the owners of Hobby Lobby in *Burwell v. Hobby Lobby Stores, Inc*?
9. What did the four dissenting justices say in response to the same-sex marriage case of *Obergefell v. Hodges*?
10. How do you think Christians should respond to Supreme Court decisions that challenge and demean the Christian faith?

Unit 9

Lesson 41

1. What does it mean for a state to extend "full faith and credit" to the other states?
2. What are some limitations to the "full faith and credit" clause?
3. What does the guarantee of privileges and immunities mean?
4. What restrictions did the Constitution place on territories concerning their becoming states?
5. What document set the pattern for territories becoming states?
6. What condition did Congress place on Utah Territory before it could become a state?
7. What provision in its state Constitution did Arizona Territory have to remove before it could become a state?
8. What area of the country became a state in spite of the restrictions the Constitution placed on territories before they became states?
9. List the five U.S. territories named in the lesson.
10. What form of government is guaranteed to the states?

Lesson 42

1. The power to amend the Constitution rests where?
2. What majority of both houses of Congress must approve an amendment before Congress submits it to the states?
3. What portion of the states must ratify an amendment before it becomes part of the Constitution?
4. What are the two most recent proposed amendments that did not receive enough state approval to become part of the Constitution?
5. Would you have supported the Equal Rights Amendment? Why or why not?
6. What is the purpose of the supremacy clause?
7. Why is an oath of office important?
8. Most people taking an oath for a federal position add what phrase to the oath of office?
9. Office holders in what three levels of government must take an oath or affirmation that they will uphold the Constitution?
10. How many states had to ratify the Constitution for it to take effect?

Lesson 43

1. What congressman edited proposals state conventions made and put them forward as twelve amendments for Congress to consider?
2. What does the Bill of Rights limit?
3. What kinds of expression does the First Amendment not protect?
4. What agency did the federal government create to regulate broadcasting?
5. Do you believe that the federal government should regulate radio and television broadcasts? Explain your answer.
6. What was the FCC's Fairness Doctrine?
7. Why was the Fairness Doctrine dropped?
8. In 1989 the Supreme Court declared an action to be protected as a First Amendment right. What was that action?
9. What is your opinion of that Supreme Court decision?
10. What issues are raised when the Ku Klux Klan applies for a permit to hold a rally?

Lesson 44

1. What did Thomas Jefferson say about the importance of the right to own and use guns?
2. What is the historical context for the second amendment?
3. Describe a twentieth century example of a government taking guns away from private citizens.
4. What is your personal position concerning gun control and the right to bear arms?
5. What is the historical context for the Third Amendment?
6. Why is it important for every citizen, even those with criminal records, to be considered innocent of a crime until proven guilty?
7. Amendments Five through Eight protect the rights of whom?
8. Do you believe that the death penalty is "cruel and unusual punishment"?
9. What did Alexander Hamilton fear about the Bill of Rights?
10. What does the Tenth Amendment say?

Lesson 45

1. What did the Thirteenth Amendment do and which states did Congress require to ratify it?
2. What are the main provisions of the Fourteenth Amendment?
3. What did the Fourteenth Amendment forbid former federal and state office holders who had participated in the rebellion of the Confederacy from doing?
4. List two examples of ways states hindered African Americans from voting even after the Fifteenth Amendment became part of the Constitution.
5. What political movement promoted the income tax as a way to generate government revenue and distribute wealth equally?
6. The only amendment ever to be repealed concerned the prohibition of what?
7. What is your opinion about Prohibition?
8. Would you have supported or opposed the Nineteenth Amendment? Why or why not?
9. What discriminatory practice did the Twenty-Fourth Amendment outlaw?
10. Which amendment passed more quickly than any other and what did it do?

Unit 10

Lesson 46

1. Which level of government has the most authority about education issues?
2. In early state constitutions, why was most of the power vested in legislatures?
3. Which was the only original state to elect a constitutional convention?
4. All state constitutions establish what three branches of government?
5. Whom does every state constitution mention?
6. What are two times in American history when states had to write new constitutions?
7. What are the major differences between state constitutions and the U.S. Constitution?
8. What state has the longest constitution at over 376,000 words?
9. In almost all states, the legislature may place amendments before whom?
10. Are voters more likely to vote on amendments to their state constitutions or to vote to elect officials?

Lesson 47

1. Where do state constitutions vest the law-making power of state governments?
2. What is every upper house in the state legislatures called?
3. State senators generally serve a term of how many years?
4. State representatives generally serve a term of how many years?
5. What is the most representative body in the world based on population?
6. What is unusual about the Nebraska state legislature?
7. How can citizens of some states bypass the typical legislative procedure to enact laws?
8. What is the most obvious difference between sessions of state legislatures and sessions of Congress?
9. What issue did the Supreme Court cases *Baker v. Carr* and *Reynolds v. Sims* address?
10. What do you think are the pros and cons of low pay for legislators versus high pay?

Lesson 48

1. Who is the chief executive of a state?
2. A governor serves as the head of what military organization?
3. What official holds the number two position in most states?
4. How do length of term and the presence or absence of term limits affect the power of a governor?
5. How does the length and frequency of legislative sessions affect the power of a governor?
6. What roles do governors fill that prepare them well for serving as president?
7. Who are four recent governors who have gone on to become president?
8. How many terms had Jimmy Carter served as governor of Georgia before he became president of the United States?
9. Who was the first governor of Texas to win election to consecutive four-year terms?
10. Do you think governors should have the ability to exercise a line-item veto? Explain your answer.

Lesson 49

1. What is meant by the term "red tape"?
2. What is the job of the secretary of state of South Dakota?
3. Who chooses department secretaries in South Dakota government?
4. What South Dakota official examines how state government spends funds in order to assure the process is accurate and efficient?
5. What is the role of the South Dakota Department of Corrections?
6. What is the purpose of the South Dakota Department of Public Safety?
7. What is the purpose of the South Dakota Department of Tribal Relations?
8. The Texas state supreme court has final appellate jurisdiction in what two types of cases?
9. What Texas court holds final appellate jurisdiction in criminal cases?
10. How do people become judges in Texas?

Lesson 50

1. Why do state governments try to encourage economic growth?
2. Most job growth within a state comes from what types of businesses?
3. What kind of tax incentives do states sometimes offer a business?
4. What types of infrastructure can state governments provide in order to help businesses be successful?
5. What is the most important asset for any company?
6. In what two ways do governors and other state officials help state economies by making official trips to foreign countries?
7. How many dollars are estimated to be spent by tourists in the United States each year?
8. How do states promote tourism?
9. What growing tourist industry is mentioned in the lesson?
10. What business would you like to start to benefit your state?

Unit 11

Lesson 51

1. What is the historic background of American county government?
2. Why do counties exist today?
3. County courthouses and county government offices are located in what city?
4. What is the most common form of county government in the U.S.?
5. What are the two other most common forms of county governments?
6. What is a township?
7. How many states have townships?
8. What kind of government do people form to provide a specific function?
9. What body usually oversees a special district?
10. Would you like to be part of your county or township government some day? If so, in what way would you like to serve?

Lesson 52

1. America has become more urban than it once was. List five advantages to living in an urban area and five advantages to living in a rural area.
2. What government entity incorporates villages, towns, and cities?
3. A city charter compares to what?
4. What was the first form of city government in America?
5. What is the most common form of city government today?
6. When candidates run on their own merits rather than as the candidates of a political party, they run on what basis?
7. What might a stadium authority do?
8. Give an example of a type of business that might receive a franchise from a city.
9. What are some advantages of a consolidated government?
10. What are some disadvantages of a consolidated government?

Lesson 53

1. What do urban planning professionals do?
2. Who made the orderly plan for Philadelphia?
3. Who made the plan for Washington, D.C.?
4. What planning movement culminated in the World's Columbian Exposition in Chicago?
5. What is a planning commission?
6. What is zoning?
7. Who oversees the zoning process?
8. What does zoning separate?
9. What happens when a city annexes property?
10. What is eminent domain?

Lesson 54

1. The economy of Williston, North Dakota, was once based on what?
2. What two national tourist sites are near Williston?
3. What is another term for fracking and how is it accomplished?
4. What type of tax does North Dakota charge oil companies?
5. What does North Dakota award oil companies through competitive bidding?
6. The oil boom caused a crisis in government in what service areas?
7. Why did Williston take on debt?
8. How did mass transportation change in Williston?
9. What services do you believe the government should provide to displaced persons in a place like Williston?
10. What services do you believe churches should provide to displaced persons in a place like Williston?

Lesson 55

1. What binds the country together on all levels of government?
2. What legislation did Thomas Jefferson encourage Congress to pass that had a negative effect on American port cities?
3. What is RFD?
4. What federal government program helped the mail order industry?
5. What were the two names of the first federal highway?
6. What is the system of numbered federal highways begun in 1926?
7. What is the system of roads begun in 1956?
8. What do federal officials use to allocate funding each year to state, local, and tribal governments?
9. How does illegal immigration affect state and local governments?
10. How did many states respond to the Supreme Court's decision in *Brown v. Board of Education*?

See page 27 for literary analysis of and questions over *Born Again*.

Literary Analysis
Born Again
by Charles Colson

Born Again is a book about power: the power of a president to do good and to do evil, the jockeying for power among his aides, the utter powerlessness that Charles Colson felt as the weight of his wrongs descended on him, his powerlessness in the world of prison life, the power of Christ to change a person's life, and the power of the fellowship of believers to help a struggling brother through the most difficult period in his life.

Colson achieved a high political position and had great influence in a presidential administration, but he lost all that and as a result took a very different course with his life. He went from working in the White House as a close adviser to the president to serving time in a federal prison with hardened criminals. Yet God used his life to accomplish much good after he lost worldly power and gained Christ.

The book is something of a history of the Nixon Administration. It describes the web of advisers who served under a complex man, who was capable of gentle kindness, brilliant diplomacy, visionary leadership, sheer dishonesty, dirty politics, and paralyzing paranoia.

When the book was published in 1976, the great majority of Americans knew about the trials of the Vietnam War followed by the catastrophe of Watergate. These events and many of the names of the people involved had been in the news every day for months. The narrative of *Born Again* had great immediacy for its first readers. They would have absorbed the detail of Colson's memories and his perspectives on the Watergate situation. He did a good job in the book of untangling the complex story. The people involved in the disasters of the Nixon Administration have faded from public awareness as a new generation has arisen; some details are not so important now. However, the central message of *Born Again*—in Christ is the power of salvation—is timeless. The setting of that message within a specific historic context demonstrates its vibrancy and credibility.

Colson's narrative begins with the 1972 election, with Nixon at the pinnacle of power and Colson about to leave his position as special counsel to the president. The scene sets the tone for the narrative that follows. Colson then uses flashback to tell about his earlier years and the pridefulness that guided his life. At one point he says that he didn't think he had failed at anything.

After serving in the Marines, Colson became an attorney and got involved in Republican politics. At the age of 38 he took the position of special counsel in Nixon's White House. This meant that he carried out various assignments for the president. He was what some people (including Colson himself) called Nixon's hatchet man. This meant that he used his position to get things done, sometimes hurting other people in the process. In print, Colson was described as being willing to run over his grandmother to get Nixon re-elected. Many people assumed that Colson himself had actually made that statement.

During his years with Nixon, Colson was involved in an attempt to discredit Daniel Ellsberg, who had made public secret documents known as the "Pentagon Papers." These documents showed a pattern of deceptive government practices from before Nixon became president. Colson's actions were all part of the dog-eat-dog political climate Colson knew well.

In the last year of Colson's service in the White House, the Watergate burglary took place. The men who broke into Democratic Party headquarters worked with contacts in the White House and on Nixon's re-election staff. Colson did not have anything to do with Watergate, but what he had done reflected the same kind of corrupt politics. Colson left the White House in early 1973 to return to private law practice. His ruthless actions and tense experiences in the Nixon Administration had left him empty and searching.

Back in legal practice, Colson became reacquainted with Tom Phillips, president of Raytheon Company and a legal client. Tom had changed since Colson had last seen him—he had come to faith in Christ. Phillips gave Colson a copy of *Mere Christianity* by C. S. Lewis, which convicted Colson of his pridefulness and pointed him toward the loving Savior and Lord. Colson soon accepted Christ.

An important theme in the book is the support Colson found in the fellowship of other Christians who stood by him in his newfound faith and through the trials he endured. Senator Harold Hughes became one of his best friends and staunchest supporters. Politically, Hughes had been a sharp critic of Nixon and Colson, but their brotherhood in Christ transcended the past.

Colson's conversion to Christ shocked many and met with widespread skepticism. Many didn't know what to make of it. Imagine hearing about someone famous for dirty political tricks (supposedly willing to run over his own grandmother) suddenly confessing faith in Christ. You might feel skeptical, too. Colson endured much ridicule in the press. He made headlines for his involvement with Nixon (including false charges regarding Watergate) even as he made headlines about his newfound faith. (Remember: just because you read or hear something in the media doesn't mean it is true.)

The Nixon Administration fell apart. Many advisers went to prison, the vice president resigned because of a different scandal, and Nixon himself resigned in August of 1974. Colson's attorney believed that he could get Colson off without going to prison, but Colson's great crisis of conscience occurred when he became convinced that he had to confess his guilt in the Ellsberg case and take whatever consequences came. His punishment was harsher than he expected, but he accepted it and went to prison.

Colson's fall from power was complete; but in prison he found strength in his faith and in the fellowship of other believers, and he tried to help other prisoners. The harsh conditions, the hardened attitudes of many inmates and jailers, and the trials of his fellow prisoners broke his heart and led to his founding Prison Fellowship, a discipleship ministry that brings help and hope to thousands of prisoners who want to start over.

Colson's later life demonstrated the genuineness of his conversion. He gave himself to Prison Fellowship, reaching out to people few others in society cared about. *Born Again* was the first of over thirty books that Colson wrote about faith, the Christian life, and apologetics. Reading any of his other books will be a blessing also.

Colson had a significant influence on evangelical Christianity and in encouraging a Christian worldview. Colson's personal and professional downfall led to his giving his life to the service of God and helping others in immeasurable ways. His life is an example of God's power to bring good out of something bad.

Note: A handful of times in *Born Again*, Colson refers to African Americans in a way that could be taken as demeaning. These references have no bearing on the story. We find these references offensive and unfortunate. Charles Colson genuinely embraced fellowship with other people, regardless of color. His narrative reflects a different time in American history, though that does not excuse disrespect. Hopefully Americans have made progress in attitudes and understanding toward people who are different, and in using respectful, honoring language. We should be sure that our references to a person's race or ethnicity are appropriate and do not come from an attitude of prejudice.

Questions on *Born Again*

Write about one page total to answer questions 1-3:

1. What did you learn about the political realm in *Born Again* that surprised you?
2. After reading about Colson's prison experiences, what do you think about the prison system? Do you think prison is effective as a punishment for crime?
3. What do you think Colson wanted the reader to come away with after reading his story?

Write about one-half to one page:

4. Write a summary and review of *Born Again*.

Unit 12

Lesson 56

1. What is a budget?
2. What do you believe should be the most essential spending priority for the federal budget?
3. What do you believe should be the most essential spending priority for your city or county's local budget?
4. What office holder proposes the federal budget to Congress?
5. What conflicts do conservatives and liberals often have concerning budgets?
6. What is a sunset law?
7. Why do government agencies try to spend all of the money in their budgets?
8. What are capital projects?
9. What spending restriction do most states have that the federal government does not?
10. What can result from a government printing money to make up a budget shortfall?

Lesson 57

1. The total debt of the federal government is approaching how many dollars?
2. What is the greatest source of revenue for the federal government?
3. Most Americans pay their income tax through what process?
4. What is a progressive tax?
5. The top one percent of Americans pay what percentage of the total income tax that the IRS collects?
6. What are some items on which the federal government collects excise taxes?
7. What does the government do when Social Security revenue exceeds benefits paid out in one year?
8. What is a government bond?
9. What is the relationship between a borrower and a lender?
10. Do you think something needs to be done about the national debt? If so, what?

Lesson 58

1. Do states or the federal government have lower income tax rates?
2. What is a sales tax?
3. What are items that are exempt from sales tax, or taxed at a lower rate, in certain states?
4. What groups generally don't have to pay sales tax on purchases they make?
5. On what is the *ad valorem* tax based when registering a vehicle?
6. What two taxes have become popular with state and local governments in recent years?
7. Why have governments found these taxes attractive?
8. What is a federal categorical grant?
9. What is a biennial budget?
10. In 2015 each adult resident of Alaska who had lived there at least one year received a dividend of $2,072 from the sale of what?

Lesson 59

1. The major portion of a county's revenue comes from what?
2. Who determines the appraised value for this?
3. When are property taxes collected?
4. Do businesses or individuals generally pay higher property tax?
5. What fee does Lexington, Kentucky, impose that is similar to an income tax?
6. What three sources of city revenue does the lesson list?
7. List in order the top three budgeted expenditures for Fairfax County, Virginia, in 2016.
8. What does Fairfax County's public safety budget item include?
9. What must people involved in collecting and spending public money be careful to do?
10. What is Tax Freedom Day?

Lesson 60

1. Why was chartering a national bank controversial?
2. When the government under the Constitution first began, citizens assumed that the federal government would exercise only what?
3. Though President Grover Cleveland believed that the people should support the government, what did he say that the government should not do?
4. What happened when President Cleveland vetoed a congressional appropriation of $10,000 to help farmers in Texas?
5. What is the proper purpose of tax policy?
6. Some people believe that governments should use taxes to influence what?
7. Some people believe that governments should use taxes to redistribute what?
8. Which generally helps the economy more, raising taxes or lowering taxes?
9. Describe two situations the lesson mentions that might justify a government borrowing money.
10. What do you think about government taxation to redistribute income?

Unit 13

Lesson 61

1. What does the word diplomacy mean?
2. The Constitution assigns the role of head of state to what person?
3. What is the role of an ambassador?
4. What is the role of a consul?
5. What term describes a government in one country believing that the government of another country is legitimate?
6. For what political reason did the United States send aid to smaller countries during the Cold War?
7. What happened at the U.S. embassy in Tehran, Iran, in the late 1970s?
8. How and why did U.S. relations change with Iran after the crisis at the U.S. embassy in Tehran?
9. Why does the United States encourage freedom and democracy in other countries?
10. If you could serve in an American embassy abroad, in what country would you like to serve and why?

Lesson 62

1. What does America's participation in international trade involve?
2. What was the major U.S. trade policy before World War II?
3. What are GATT and the WTO?
4. What is a country guaranteed if it has Normal Trade Relations status with the U.S.?
5. What are NAFTA and CAFTA?
6. What has happened to the economies of the U.S., Mexico, and Canada since the passage of NAFTA?
7. What are some negative consequences of NAFTA?
8. What changed in American trade with China between 1985 and 2015?
9. What do opponents of trade with China fear about this trend?
10. What are two ways in which governments work against free trade?

Lesson 63

1. One terrorist attack triggered a war on terrorism in Afghanistan and Iraq. When did it take place?
2. That event triggered a war on the forces of terrorism in what two countries?
3. Define state sponsors of terrorism.
4. What illegal activity does the lesson suggest might fund terrorism?
5. Why does the U.S. government engage in diplomacy to fight terrorism?
6. What does the lesson mention as purposes of secret operations?
7. What international organization gathers information about terrorists?
8. How might the U.S. government invade the privacy of American citizens to obtain information about possible terrorists?
9. Federal officials working against terrorism must investigate the transfer of what?
10. What is the real answer to terrorism and hatred?

Lesson 64

1. What did George Washington believe was a "baneful foe of republican government"?
2. Washington said that if a nation has habitual hatred or habitual fondness for another nation, it is in some degree a what?
3. What international organization did President Woodrow Wilson promote after World War I?
4. What international body did the United States help to create after World War II?
5. What five countries are permanent members of the U.N. Security Council?
6. The lesson mentions three of the U.N.'s many agencies. What are they?
7. Name two times when the United Nations has helped the United States with an international problem.
8. What key alliance did the U.S. and eleven other countries form after World War II?
9. When and where did NATO military forces first enter combat?
10. Do you favor U.S. isolationism or major involvement in the affairs of other nations in the world? Why?

Lesson 65

1. How are human rights defined in the lesson?
2. What are three negative consequences of boycotting countries which violate human rights?
3. What did Presidents Reagan and Bush do as they carried on talks and engaged in relations with the Soviet Union?
4. What term is often used for racial segregation in South Africa?
5. When did America restore diplomatic relations with Cuba?
6. The lesson mentions three types of human rights violations in China. What are they?
7. What should be the response of a Christian who learns that an American company is purchasing products from factories where people work in terrible conditions?
8. What was the term once used to describe what is now called human trafficking?
9. How does Christianity differ from religions that teach people to hate their enemies?
10. If you were appointed to work on the federal level in a position that involved human rights, what would be your first priority?

Unit 14

Lesson 66

1. What is an economy?
2. Define a free market economy.
3. Define a command economy.
4. A free market economy is sometimes called what?
5. Describe a regulated free market economy.
6. Why do capitalists need regulation?
7. Who operates the Amtrak passenger rail service?
8. What two large industries does the British government control?
9. What are three failings of a command economy?
10. What has history demonstrated time and again about economic freedom?

Lesson 67

1. The lesson states that illegal immigration is a crisis in what four areas?
2. List three types of visa.
3. What must an immigrant apply for if he or she wishes to live in the United States?
4. The 675,000 legal immigrants allowed to come to the United States each year are in what three categories?
5. What is the country of origin for most legal permanent resident applicants?
6. Underground networks apparently exist to recruit whom?
7. What are some reasons refugees leave their homes and seek asylum in another country?
8. What is political asylum?
9. List the countries from which your ancestors immigrated to America.
10. Do you think a better wall on the U.S./Mexico border is a worthwhile investment? Why or why not?

Lesson 68

1. What two federal government programs started paying for health care costs for some Americans in the 1960s?
2. Federal, state, and local governments pay for what portion of all health care costs in America?
3. What is Medicare?
4. What is Medicaid?
5. What has happened to health care costs since the federal government began to pay a large percentage of those costs?
6. President Obama proposed and Congress passed what health care legislation in 2010?
7. How have health insurance premiums changed since Congress passed this legislation?
8. What is a single-payer health care system?
9. How do government limits on medical costs affect availability of health care?
10. What health care changes do you think would benefit American society?

Lesson 69

1. In *Pierce v. Society of Sisters*, the U.S. Supreme Court ruled that a child is not a mere creature of what?
2. What were the earliest organized schools in the U.S., and how were they funded?
3. What early educational leader in Massachusetts encouraged removing religious instruction from public schools?
4. What did Mann and others see as the purpose for education?
5. What two factors decreased parental influence in children's education?
6. What event in 1957 prompted the federal government to assume greater control of education?
7. How much does government currently spend on education in the U.S.?
8. What has been the trend in federal court decisions regarding the rights of parents to influence their children's education in public schools?
9. What law passed in 2002 gave the federal government more control over public education?
10. Homeschooling is legal in how many states?

Lesson 70

1. President Ronald Reagan said that abortion is supported by whom?
2. How many babies have been aborted in the United States since 1973?
3. A 2015 video revealed Planned Parenthood officials talking flippantly about what?
4. How is abortion a spiritual issue?
5. What 1973 Supreme Court decision declared that a woman had the right to obtain an abortion?
6. What later Supreme Court decision, while upholding the right to an abortion, upheld all of the Pennsylvania restrictions except the requirement that a married woman had to notify her husband?
7. The Hyde Amendment prevents the federal government from doing what?
8. In 2007 the Supreme Court upheld what ban enacted by Congress in 2003?
9. How are abortion laws an example of legislating morality?
10. How can you help influence the moral perceptions of others?

Unit 15

Lesson 71

1. What is the origin of the phrase "wall of separation"?
2. What was Jefferson's thinking about that "wall of separation"?
3. What characteristics of the American people have the Supreme Court recognized?
4. What is the policy called release time instruction?
5. The Supreme Court has made a distinction between what two ways that the state can give assistance that relates to religion and schools?
6. What practices in New York and Pennsylvania public schools did the Supreme Court declare to be unconstitutional?
7. What did Chief Justice William Rehnquist write regarding whether the phrase "one nation under God" in the Pledge of Allegiance is patriotic or religious?
8. Judge Roy Moore has twice served as chief justice of the Alabama Supreme Court and has twice been suspended. What were the two religious freedom issues involved?
9. The Supreme Court ruled that Bob Jones University was not entitled to tax-exempt status because of what policy?
10. Do you think the Supreme Court erred in any of the rulings mentioned in this lesson? If so, name one and tell why.

Lesson 72

1. Make a list of five things you would like the congressman from your district and the senators from your state to work to reform.
2. List five things you would like to hear a presidential candidate propose in relation to reforming government.

Lesson 73

1. Choose one topic that is important to you and write a draft of an email you would like to send to your congressman or to one of your senators. If your parents approve, send it.
2. If the president appointed you to be in his Cabinet, in which department would you like to serve?
3. If you could serve as an employee in government, what job would you like to have?
4. Write a slogan you could use in a campaign to be elected as mayor.
5. If you run for public office, people have to learn about you. Make a list of five things you stand for that you could use in campaign advertising.
6. If you decided to join a political party today, which party would you choose to be in and why?
7. If you would rather not join a political party, explain why you would rather be an Independent.
8. If you were working behind the scenes in a political campaign, what job would you be most comfortable doing?
9. List three ways someone could destroy his or her reputation.
10. Write two sentences explaining why it is important for someone who works with people to have wisdom.

Lesson 74

1. The lesson tells four things America's founders believed in. List them.
2. Because our country is not perfect, what is the responsibility of each generation?
3. Americans have the freedom to educate children as they think best. Tell one reason you are thankful that your parents have chosen the method they have for your education.
4. What is one way you could have a better influence on others for good?
5. What is one way you could do a better job of not allowing the world to influence you for evil?
6. What is one way you could improve on the way you show respect to leaders?
7. Why did Henry David Thoreau refuse to pay taxes?
8. What did Jeremiah tell the exiles in Babylon to do in the city in which they lived?
9. In Matthew 5, Jesus tells us to let our light shine before men for what reason?
10. Where is a Christian's most important citizenship?

Lesson 75

1. Why did Margaret Thatcher say she was in politics?
2. Answer this question the lesson poses: If people cannot be trusted, why should you trust bureaucrats who get paid the same regardless of what happens to you?
3. Which do you prefer: security or freedom? Why?

See page 37 for literary analysis of and questions over *God and Ronald Reagan*.

Literary Analysis
God and Ronald Reagan
by Paul Kengor

Ronald Reagan was an important and influential president. He has also generated a publishing industry. One estimate holds that writers have produced over one thousand books on Reagan. Is there anything left to say? Are all these books attempts to capitalize on a great American's career? Surprisingly, one topic that writers have not examined extensively is Reagan's personal religious faith.

Paul Kengor has contributed to this collection of Reagan books with several of his own. He has also written about the faith of George W. Bush and Hillary Clinton and about other topics. Kengor is a professor of political science at Grove City College (GCC) in Pennsylvania and the director of the Center for Vision and Values at GCC. He has written numerous scholarly and popular articles and has appeared on many television news programs.

Kengor relates in *God and Ronald Reagan* that he was researching for a book about Reagan's policy toward the Soviet Union when he realized the depth and breadth of the president's faith in God and how that played a part in Reagan's thinking. The more he dug, the more he realized how all-encompassing Reagan's faith was. Rather than finishing the book he was planning, Kengor reversed the topics. He instead wrote this book about Reagan's faith, a major portion of which involves the role that his faith played in his policy toward the Soviet Union.

One must understand the faith of Ronald Reagan to understand Reagan as a person and as president. Kengor shows how Reagan's faith influenced his entire life. He notes how it informed Reagan's views on abortion, but the main point of the book is that Reagan's beliefs deeply affected his outlook on Communism. Reagan's approach was not simplistic. He condemned the U.S.S.R. as an evil, atheistic empire, and he built up American military strength; but he also showed a willingness to negotiate with the Russians. Reagan believed that the United States had a "rendezvous with destiny" to be a beacon of political freedom and the gospel of Christ. The cumulative effect was a weakening of the Soviet empire, which resulted in its downfall during the presidency of Reagan's successor, George H. W. Bush.

Throughout most of the book, Kengor emphasizes that Reagan's faith was genuine. Reagan's mother Nelle taught and modeled for her son a deep and active faith. Her strong faith made a huge impression on Reagan. He had other influences, including ministers he knew and the reading of the novel *That Printer of Udell's*. The Christian faith became his own. Because of his father's alcoholism and inability to hold a job, the Reagans moved frequently. Kengor suggests at one point that Reagan's faith filled an inner hole of loneliness that the young man felt because of this rootlessness. However, God was much more than a stopgap for Reagan. The author shows through many examples the importance of prayer for Reagan. After the attempt on his life early in his presidency, Reagan resolved to live whatever days he had left to honor God. Some have found it confusing that Reagan seldom attended church services while he was president. He was motivated out of concern for others. After the assassination attempt, he feared that going to church would put others at risk. Reagan missed attending services and resumed after he left office.

Kengor traces Reagan's anti-Communist stance from the post-World War II period when Communists infiltrated the movie industry, through his days as a spokesman for General Electric, and into his years in elective office. Reagan sprinkled his speeches with references to

God. His opposition to Communism centered on the political system's atheism, its destruction of political and personal freedom, and the determination of Communists from the time of Lenin forward to wipe out capitalism and religion around the world. The author notes that for Reagan, the conflict between democracy and Communism was nothing less than the conflict between good and evil. Kengor notes the impact of the book *Witness* by Whittaker Chambers on Reagan. (This is a large and challenging book that you might want to take on as an adult but probably aren't ready for yet.)

Reagan's 1983 speech in which he referred to the Soviet Union as the evil empire is a major point of the book. Reagan said exactly what he wanted to say and what he believed he needed to say. Liberals criticized the speech mercilessly. As it turned out, information that became available many years later revealed how evil the Soviet government was. Many in Russia at the time and later agreed with Reagan and were glad that he said it. In sum, Reagan was absolutely right in what he said and in the decision to say it.

The last major section of the book concerns Reagan's visit to Moscow in 1988. There the president spoke freely about God and expressed his desire for freedom and faith to blossom in the Soviet Union. His visit opened the door even further for the fall of Communism in Eastern Europe and in the Soviet Union that occurred over the next three years.

One matter that Kengor leaves unresolved is the faith of Mikhail Gorbachev. As leader of the officially atheist Soviet Union, Gorbachev kept a public distance from religion but made occasional comments suggesting an openness to God. Later, in other settings, Gorbachev has declared that he is a Christian and that he believes he was God's chosen man to lead the Soviet Union out of Godless Communism once a leader arose in the United States who would not take advantage of Russia's collapse.

In his book, Kengor makes some astute observations about Reagan's life. He says that Reagan had a pretty typical youth but anything but a typical adulthood. He parallels Reagan's growing-up years with events taking place in the Soviet Union at the same time, a literary device that prepares us for the dramatic confrontation between Reagan and the Soviets during Reagan's presidency. He says that Reagan's faith was the most active and meaningful at the "bookends" of Reagan's life, meaning his boyhood years and in his last public role as president. Kengor reveals a good grasp of the Disciples of Christ movement and the influence of Alexander Campbell.

Notes: The book never explains the origin of Reagan's nickname Dutch. The story is that when Ronald was born, his father said that the baby looked like a fat little Dutchman; and the nickname stuck. On page 20 the author refers to Philippians 4:8 as Christ's words, but Paul wrote Philippians.

Reagan was convinced that God has a plan for the world, for the United States, for his own life, and for all lives. This inspired and motivated Reagan. May we be motivated and inspired by the same faith.

Questions on *God and Ronald Reagan*

Write about one page total to answer questions 1-3:

1. How would you describe Reagan's faith?
2. Describe the ways you think Ronald Reagan is a positive example for those in public office.
3. Reagan saw the Cold War primarily as a spiritual conflict, not a political, economic, or military conflict. Do you think this applies to issues in our world (such as the war on Islamic terrorism, the decline of marriage, and the acceptance of same-sex relationships) in the same way--as at root spiritual issues that require spiritual answers?

Write about one-half to one page:

4. Write a summary and review of *God and Ronald Reagan*.